READING POWER

Cobi Jones
Soccer Star

Rob Kirkpatrick

The Rosen Publishing Group's
PowerKids Press ™
New York

To the teachers who made school fun.

Published in 2000 by The Rosen Publishing Group, Inc.
29 East 21st Street, New York, NY 10010

First Edition

Book design: Maria Melendez

Photo Credits: p. 5 © Ken White/Allsport; p. 7 © Jamie Squire/Allsport; p. 9 © Brian Bahr/Allsport; p. 11 © Stephen Dunn/Allsport; p. 13 © Rick Stewart/Allsport; pp. 15, 22 courtesy of UCLA Sports Information Department; p. 17 © Aubrey Washington/Allsport; p. 19 © Jonathan Daniel/Allsport; p. 21 © Ken White/Allsport.

Text Consultant: Linda J. Kirkpatrick, Reading Specialist/Reading Recovery Teacher

Kirkpatrick, Rob.
Cobi Jones: soccer star/by Rob Kirkpatrick.
p. cm.—(Reading power)
Includes index.
SUMMARY: Introduces Cobi Jones, star player for the Los Angeles Galaxy soccer team.
ISBN 0-8239-5540-0
1. Jones, Cobi Juvenile literature. 2. Soccer players—United States Biography Juvenile literature. [1. Jones, Cobi. 2. Soccer players.] I. Title. II. Series.
GV942.7.J66 K57 1999
796.334'092—dc21
[B]
99-16066
CIP

Manufactured in the United States of America

Contents

Cobi Jones plays soccer.

13

Cobi plays for the Los Angeles Galaxy.

GALAXY
LOS ANGELES
GALAXY

Soccer players kick the ball to move it. This is called dribbling. Cobi likes to dribble.

4
13
Bud

The ball can go in the air.
Then Cobi can hit it with
his head.

GALAXY
13

Cobi plays soccer all the time. He even plays when it is wet and cold.

GALAXY
13
Bud

Cobi went to school at U.C.L.A. He played soccer at U.C.L.A.

Cobi has played for the United States team.

Soccer players can get tired when they play.

Bud
13

Cobi is happy when he scores a goal. He runs around when he scores.

JONES
Budweiser

Cobi loves soccer.

Here are more books to read about Cobi Jones and soccer:

Cobi Jones: Soccer Games
by Cobi Jones, Andrew Gutelle,
illustrated by Paul Meisel
Workman Publishing (1998)

Soccer Game! (Hello Reader!)
by Grace MacCarone, illustrated by
Meredith Johnson
Scholastic Trade (1994)

This Is Soccer
by Margaret Blackstone, illustrated by
John O'Brien
Henry Holt & Company, Inc. (1999)

To learn more about soccer, check out this Web site:
http://sportsline.netscape.com/ns/soccer/index/html

Glossary

dribble (DRIH-bul) When a soccer player moves the ball with his feet.

goal (GOHL) When a player puts the ball in the net and scores a point.

team (TEEM) A group of players.

Index

Word Count: 101

Note to Librarians, Teachers, and Parents

If reading is a challenge, Reading Power is a solution! Reading Power is perfect for readers who want high-interest subject matter at an accessible reading level. These fact-filled, photo-illustrated books are designed for readers who want straightforward vocabulary, engaging topics, and a manageable reading experience. With clear picture/text correspondence, leveled Reading Power books put the reader in charge. Now readers have the power to get the information they want and the skills they need in a user-friendly format.